Dinosaur Nests

Written by Jo Windsor

Illustrated by Dave Gunson

In this book
you will see
dinosaurs.

You will see...

dinosaur nests

dinosaur eggs

baby dinosaurs

This dinosaur lived a long time ago.
It lived with lots and lots of dinosaurs.

This is a mother dinosaur.

She has a big head.
She has a big tail.
She has a big body.

The mother is digging.

Is she making a nest?

Yes. The mother dinosaur is making a nest.

The nest is...

for eggs   Yes? No?

for sleeping in   Yes? No?

for eating in   Yes? No?

Look at the nest.
It is on the ground.
The nest is made of dirt.

What has the dinosaur made the nest for?

She has made a nest for her eggs.

The eggs will be...

baby birds   **Yes? No?**

baby fish   **Yes? No?**

baby dinosaurs **Yes? No?**

Look at all the eggs.
The mother dinosaur has lots
and lots of eggs in her nest.

She puts leaves and
grass on top of the eggs.
The dinosaur eggs are under
the leaves and grass.

The leaves and grass will help
keep the eggs warm.

The eggs are warm...

so they will cook   Yes? No?

so the babies
will grow   Yes? No?

The eggs are warm.
The baby dinosaurs will grow.

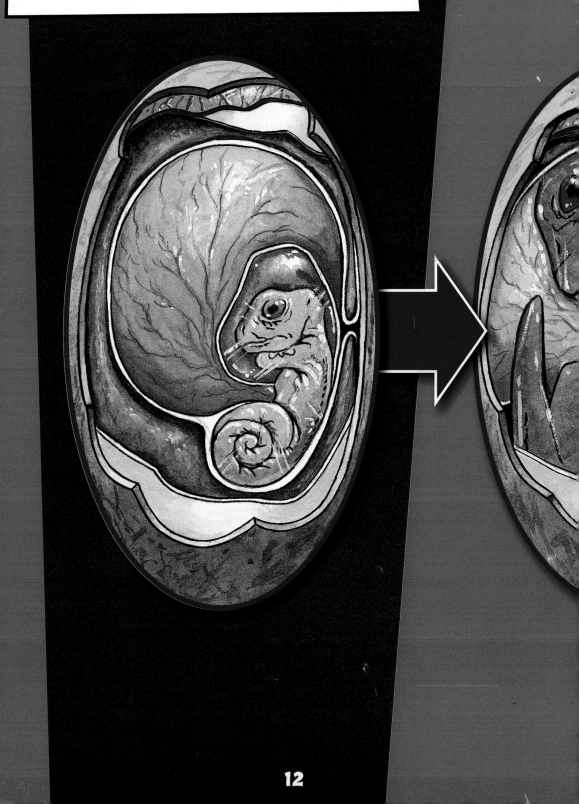

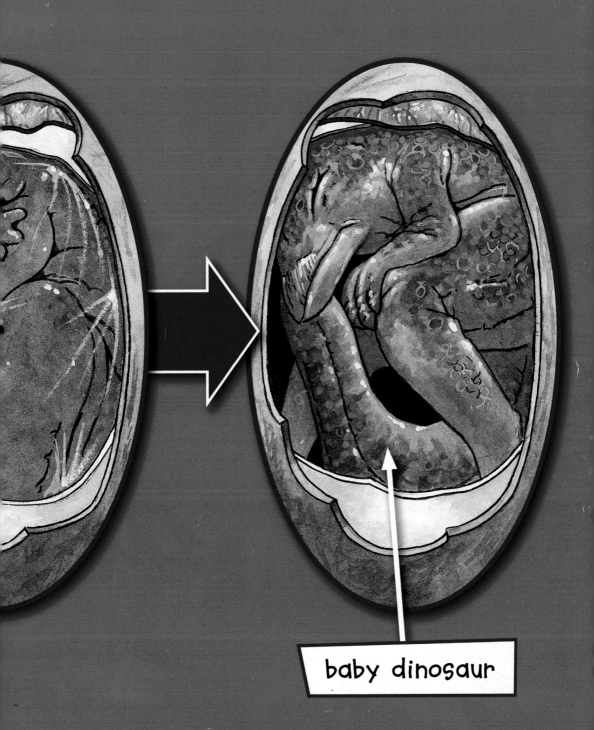

baby dinosaur

The mother and father dinosaur stay by the nest.

They stay by the nest to keep the eggs safe.

The eggs are safe from...

fish   Yes? No?

dinosaurs   Yes? No?

me   Yes? No?

Look!
The baby dinosaurs are coming out of the eggs.

The babies are little.
The mother and father are very big.

The mother and father will...

get food for the the babies	Yes? No?
put the babies out of the nest	Yes? No?
eat the babies	Yes? No?

The baby dinosaurs stay in the nest.

The mother dinosaur will look after the babies.

The baby dinosaurs
are growing very fast.

When they are big,
they will go out of the nest.

Index

It goes
like
this.

Yes? No?

Word Bank

body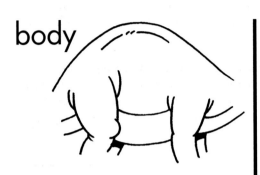

leaves

grass

nest

head

tail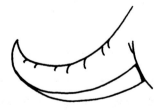